COUNTRY PROFILE: BOLIVIA

COUNTRY

Formal Name: Republic of Bolivia (República de Bolivia).

Short Form: Bolivia.

Term for Citizen(s): Bolivian(s).

Capitals: La Paz (executive) and Sucre (judicial).

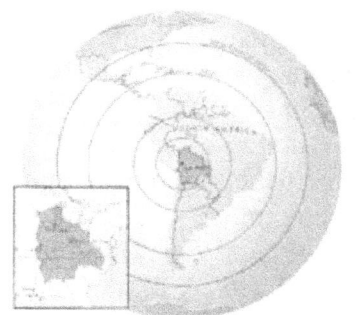

Click to Enlarge Image

Major Cities: Santa Cruz (1.3 million inhabitants), Cochabamba (900,000), El Alto (830,000), La Paz (810,000), and Sucre (225,000), according to 2005 projections.

Independence: Led by "El Libertador," Simón Bolívar Palacios, Bolivia gained complete independence from Spanish and Peruvian control in 1825. Despite nearly 200 coups and counter-coups, Bolivia has maintained its autonomy since independence.

Public Holidays: The following are Bolivia's federal holidays: New Year's Day (January 1), Carnival (two days, variable dates in February or March), Good Friday (variable date in March or April), Labor Day (May 1), Corpus Christi (variable date in May or June), Independence Day (August 6), All Saints' Day (November 1), Christmas (December 25). Each of Bolivia's nine departments also has a holiday celebrating its inception.

Flag: The Bolivian flag is divided into three equal, horizontal bands of red, yellow, and green. The Bolivian coat of arms is centered in the middle yellow band.

Click to Enlarge Image

HISTORICAL BACKGROUND

Pre-colonial and Colonial Era: Advanced Indian societies inhabited the Andes region of South America long before the arrival of Europeans. Ruins of these societies, especially the Tiwanaku civilization, dot the high-altitude Bolivian countryside, serving as reminders of the first great Andean empire. Tiwanakan dominance lasted until 1200, when the regional kingdoms of the Aymara subsequently emerged as the most powerful of the ethnic groups living in the densely populated region surrounding Lake Titicaca. Power struggles continued until 1450, when the Incas incorporated upper Bolivia into their growing empire. Based in present-day Peru, the Incas instituted agriculture and mining practices that rivaled those put in place many years later by European conquerors. They also established a strong military force and centralized political power. Despite their best efforts, however, the Incas never completely controlled nomadic tribes of the Bolivian lowlands, nor did they fully assimilate the Aymara kingdoms into their society. These internal divisions doomed the Inca Empire when European conquerors arrived.

Francisco Pizarro and his fellow Spanish conquistadors first glimpsed the "New World" in 1524. Visions of a land of gold led to aggressive colonization. Even without the arrival of the Europeans, the Inca Empire was floundering. Pizarro enjoyed stunning initial success in his military campaign against the Incas. After initial defeats, the Incas rallied some resistance against the Europeans. But in 1538, the Spaniards defeated Inca forces near Lake Titicaca, allowing penetration into central and southern Bolivia. Although Indian resistance continued, Spanish imperialists pushed forward, founding La Paz in 1549 and Santa Cruz de la Sierra (hereafter, Santa Cruz) in 1561. In the region then known as Upper Peru, the Spaniards found the mineral treasure chest they had been searching for. Potosí had the Western world's largest concentration of silver. At its height in the sixteenth century, Potosí supported a population of more than 150,000, making it the world's largest urban center. In the 1570s, Viceroy Francisco de Toledo introduced a coercive form of labor, the *mita*, which required Indian males from highland districts to spend every sixth year working in the mines. The *mita*, along with technological advances in refining, caused mining at Potosí to flourish.

Breakdown of Colonial Authority: In the early eighteenth century, the mining industry entered a prolonged period of decline, as evidenced by the eclipsing of Potosí by La Paz. After 1700, only small amounts of bullion were shipped from Upper Peru to Spain. In the mid-eighteenth century, Spanish control over South America began to weaken. In 1780 the Inca descendant, Túpac Amaru II, led nearly 60,000 Indians against the Spaniards near the Peruvian city of Cuzco. Spain put down the revolt in 1783 and executed thousands of Indians as punishment, but the revolt illustrated the precarious nature of Spanish colonial rule in the Andes.

The invasion of the Iberian Peninsula in 1807 by Napoleon Bonaparte and its aftermath further undermined Spain's authority. Although many elites in Upper Peru stayed loyal to Spain, others began to seek independence. On May 25, 1809, radical criollos of Upper Peru led one of Latin America's first independence revolts. Although defeated, the radicals set the stage for more successful rebellions. After July 1809, Spain never again fully controlled Upper Peru. The region became the battleground for a seven-year struggle between royalist troops from Peru and the forces of the independent Argentine Republic. By 1817 the royalists, based in Lima, had suppressed Argentina's independence fighters seeking to wrest Bolivia from Spanish control. It proved to be only a temporary victory. In 1820 conflict reemerged in Upper Peru among three groups: loyalists, who accepted the direction of the Spanish Cortes; rebels, led by Simón Bolívar Palacios; and Conservative Party criollos, led by General Pedro Antonio de Olañeta, who refused to join either royalist forces or the rebel war effort. Bolívar's victory over royal troops at the Battle of Ayacucho in 1824, followed by the assassination of Olañeta by his own men on April 1, 1825, brought to an end Spanish rule in Upper Peru.

Early Republic: Bolívar left the inhabitants of Upper Peru to determine the details of their own independence, transferring authority to General Antonio José de Sucre Alcalá. In August 1825, a constituent assembly convoked by Sucre rejected attachment to either Peru or Argentina and passed a resolution of independence. In an attempt to placate Bolívar's reservations regarding the country's fitness for self-rule, the new nation became known as the Republic of Bolivia.

Bolívar served five months as Bolivia's first president before being succeeded by Sucre in January 1826. The new country faced many challenges, including numerous boundary disputes with its neighbors, a moribund silver mining industry, lack of foreign credit, and conflict with the Roman Catholic Church. In 1828 Sucre was forced from office by an invading Peruvian army seeking to reunite the two territories. The ousted president redeemed himself by defeating a Peruvian force at the Battle of Tarqui in February 1829. In May Sucre was succeeded as president by Andrés de Santa Cruz y Calahumana (1829–39), who forged a voluntary political union of Peru and Bolivia in the short-lived Peru-Bolivian Confederacy (1836–39). Santa Cruz's tenure ended in January 1839 with the defeat of the Peru-Bolivian Confederacy by a Chilean expeditionary force at the Battle of Yungay.

Mid-nineteenth-century Bolivia was beset by political instability and the rule of authoritarian strongmen, economic stagnation, and a growing sense of geographic isolation. During the authoritarian government of Manuel Isidoro Belzú Humérez (1848–55), for example, the country endured 42 attempted coups. In an effort to gain access to the main routes of transoceanic trade, in 1867 Bolivia ceded more than 100,000 square kilometers of territory to Brazil in exchange for riverine access to the Atlantic Ocean.

War of the Pacific and Aftermath: An ongoing dispute between Bolivia and Chile over the mineral-rich coast of the Atacama Desert resulted in the War of the Pacific. A tentative peace, established in 1874, proved temporary. In 1879 Bolivia, in alliance with Peru, declared war against Chile, which had previously landed troops in the contested area. Chile won a decisive victory, forcing Bolivia from the entire coastal area in 1880. In 1904 Bolivia officially ceded the coastal territory to Chile under the Treaty of Peace and Friendship. In the most traumatic episode in its history, Bolivia's path to the Pacific Ocean was lost. More than a century later, the perceived injustice of Bolivia's landlocked status remains a prevailing theme in Bolivian nationalist sentiment.

From 1880 to the 1920s, Bolivia recovered from its defeat while simultaneously witnessing the rebirth of silver mining and the growth of the tin industry. Politically, the Conservative Party dominated national politics until its overthrow by the Liberal Party in the "Federal Revolution" of 1899. A new political force, the Republican Party, came to power through a bloodless coup in 1920, but the Great Depression of the early 1930s cut short Bolivia's economic recovery.

The Chaco War: In 1932 a border dispute again turned into full-fledged war. Bolivia and Paraguay both claimed the Chaco region—a largely undeveloped area that had been the site of some oil discoveries. A series of border incidents led to broken diplomatic relations and then war. President Daniel Salamanca (1931–34) believed that the Bolivian army, trained by Germans and well armed, would overwhelm the smaller Paraguayan force. In actuality, Paraguay won all the major battles of the three-year war and drove Bolivian forces nearly 500 kilometers back into the Andes. Opponents of the war overthrew Salamanca in 1934, but it was too late to change the outcome. Bolivia suffered nearly 65,000 deaths and lost the Chaco region.

World War II and Postwar Governments: Following the humiliating defeat of the Chaco War, and in the midst of the global economic depression of the early 1930s, Bolivian governments looked inward in their efforts to promote economic development. After coming to power in 1936 through a military coup, Colonel David Toro Ruilova (1936–37) introduced a program of "military socialism." Among other measures, Toro nationalized the holdings of U.S.-owned Standard Oil. Although Toro fell victim to a military coup in 1937, subsequent leaders continued many of his statist economic policies. During World War II, Bolivia repaired relations with the United States and compensated Standard Oil for losses incurred in the nationalization. In the early postwar era, which coincided with the beginning of the Cold War, Bolivia reaffirmed its alliance with the United States and embraced the cause of anticommunism. Domestically, Conservative-led governments sought to stem the growth of the left and contain growing labor unrest. However, they failed to reverse the inflationary economic policies that were inflicting severe hardship on much of the population.

The Bolivian Revolution, 1952–64: The Nationalist Revolutionary Movement (Movimiento Nacionalista Revolucionario—MNR) ushered in Bolivia's nationalist "revolution" on April 9, 1952, when it launched an armed takeover of La Paz by mine workers in collaboration with disaffected elements of the National Police. Movement leader Víctor Paz Estenssoro assumed the presidency after a brief struggle. Begun as populist opposition party in the wake of the Chaco War, the MNR was a loose coalition of mine workers, Indian subsistence farmers, and middle-class mestizos. Once in power, the MNR moved quickly to establish its populist credentials, decreeing universal suffrage, nationalizing mining and export industries, and reapportioning large tracts of farmland among Indian smallholders. Initially, the MNR governments garnered multi-class support, but rampant inflation and declining farm productivity resulting from inadequate capital investment in agriculture held back economic growth. In 1964 Paz Estenssoro ran for and won re-election, only to be deposed by armed forces members concerned over the threat of Cuban-style revolutionary violence in the Andes. Although fundamental changes remained in place, many observers on the left lamented that the Bolivian revolution remained as yet "unfinished."

Military Rule, 1964–82: The army takeover of the government in 1964 ushered in a prolonged period of authoritarian military rule. Throughout the 1960s and 1970s, successive military governments focused on maintaining internal order, modernizing the mining sector, and vigorously defending Bolivian sovereignty. Espousing a program of "revolutionary nationalism," General Alfredo Ovando Candía (co-president, May 1965–January 1966; president, January–August 1966, 1969–70) outlined the "Revolutionary Mandate of the Armed Forces." According to Ovando, the only way to end Bolivia's underdevelopment was to allow, and encourage, the military to manage the economy and intervene in domestic politics. In October 1967, the armed forces scored a major victory when a Bolivian ranger battalion captured Argentine revolutionary Ernesto "Che" Guevara and a small band of guerrillas in the remote Villagrande region. The guerrilla band, dispatched from Havana, had tried unsuccessfully to incite a peasant rebellion among Bolivia's majority Indian population.

The 1970s were dominated by the figure of General Hugo Banzer (president, 1971–78). During its first few years, Banzer's populist military government enjoyed the support of the MNR and oversaw rapid economic growth, driven largely by heavy demand for Bolivia's commodity exports. By 1974, however, the governing coalition had splintered, and labor unrest intensified as the economy experienced a slowdown. These events prompted the military regime to resort to greater repression to maintain political control.

In the late 1970s, Bolivia's military regime came under pressure from the United States and Europe to liberalize and restore civilian democratic rule. With international pressure and opposition from civilian groups mounting, General Banzer announced a presidential election for 1980. However, two subsequent coups in the midst of congressional and presidential elections delayed the transition schedule. In September 1982, the military finally handed over the government to a civilian administration led by Hernán Silas Zuazo (president, 1982–85) of the Democratic and Popular Unity (Unidad Democrática y Popular—UDP) coalition.

Economic Crisis and the "Pacted Democracy": In the early 1980s, Bolivia faced the most severe economic crisis of the preceding three decades. The economy was beset by chronic balance of payments and fiscal deficits and a foreign debt of nearly US$3 billion. The Siles Zuazo government attempted to address Bolivia's economic crisis by negotiating several tentative stabilization programs with the International Monetary Fund (IMF). However, during the first half of 1985, the international tin market collapsed and Bolivia's inflation reached an annual rate of more than 24,000 percent. As the crisis intensified, the opposition forced Siles Zuazo to give up power through a new round of elections held in July 1985.

The 1985 presidential race became a head-to-head contest between former military dictator Banzer and MNR founder Paz Estenssoro. After luring the left-wing Movement of the Revolutionary Left (Movimiento de la Izquierda Revolucionaria—MIR) with promises of state patronage, Paz Estenssoro was elected president of Bolivia for the fourth time since 1952. Abandoning his left-wing allies and his own populist past, Paz Estenssoro decreed one of the most austere economic stabilization packages ever implemented in Latin America. Hailed as the New Economic Policy (Nueva Política Económica—NPE), the decree aimed at ending Bolivia's record-setting hyperinflation and dismantling many of the large and inefficient state enterprises that had been created by the revolution. Although successful in ending hyperinflation, the NPE brought about a sharp reduction in real wages for workers and temporarily increased the country's already high levels of poverty.

In the political realm, Paz Estenssoro and Banzer negotiated a formal power-sharing agreement, the Pact for Democracy, creating a mechanism to overcome the fragmentation of the political party system and allowing the government to push forward with its austerity measures. The pact played an important role in resolving other political impasses during the 1989 and 1993 presidential elections, in which no single candidate could claim a majority of the vote. The coalition government of President Jaime Paz Zamora (1989–93) provided continuity with the market reform policies of its predecessor and oversaw a modest economic recovery, aided by a rebound in the tin market and the discovery of vast reserves of natural gas.

The 1993 presidential election saw Paz Estenssoro's former planning minister and prominent businessman Gonzalo Sánchez de Lozada receive a plurality of the vote on the MNR ticket. Sánchez de Lozada represented a new generation of MNR leaders firmly committed to the modernization of Bolivia with the aid of private capital investment from abroad. In a policy known as "capitalization," private capital and expertise were attracted to the hydrocarbons sector. In exchange for 30-year operating contracts, foreign investors doubled the capital of state energy companies and embarked on aggressive gas exploration. As a consequence of renewed investment, known natural gas reserves increased almost fivefold by 2000, and the Bolivian state received more than US$500 million per year in royalties.

The 1997 elections saw the return of Hugo Banzer to the presidency as a civilian. Despite his campaign promises to halt privatization, Banzer continued most of the economic policies of his predecessor. The retired general also embarked on a campaign to halt the illicit export of coca, the primary ingredient of cocaine, and a cause for concern in the United States. Coca farming has existed in parts of Bolivia since Inca times, but it took on increased importance and spread to new areas of the country as the international drug trade expanded during the 1980s and 1990s. Pressure from the United States to curb coca production led the Banzer administration to implement the Dignity Plan, an aggressive program of crop eradication by the Bolivian armed forces. Although temporarily successful in its limited aims of eradicating coca fields, the Dignity Plan increased rural poverty and sparked a new generation of social protest movements among the largely indigenous coca farmers (*cocaleros*) of the Chapare region.

Regionalism, Identity Politics, and the "Crisis of Governance": New social movements founded on regionalism and ethnic identity emerged as a major force in Bolivian politics during the latter part of the Banzer administration. The discovery of vast reserves of natural gas in the late 1990s provoked a heated controversy over ownership of natural resources and the extent to which Bolivia should pursue "neo-liberal" economic policies favorable to foreign capital investment. The debate pitted the natural gas-rich eastern province of Santa Cruz against social movements that drew much of their support from the poorer communities of central and western Bolivia. Encompassing a variety of groups, such as shantytown dwellers, indigenous communities, and *cocaleros*, the social movements claimed to represent Bolivians who had suffered discrimination and exclusion from the country's mainstream political and economic institutions. Common themes among the social movements were a strong anticapitalist bias and an affinity for socialism, nationalism (as expressed in anti-U.S. and anti-Chilean sentiment), and a deep-seated suspicion of foreign corporations involved in Bolivian joint ventures and privatizations. The social movements distinguished themselves from political parties by encouraging disruptive forms of protest, such as road blockades and occupations of government buildings. A key incident that galvanized opposition to the government was the so-called "water war," in which the social movements in the city of Cochabamba vigorously disputed the concession of a commercial waterworks contract to the Bechtel Corporation on the grounds that the poor would be deprived of universal access to water.

In May 2001, President Banzer resigned from office because of a terminal illness. A caretaker administration under Vice President Jorge Quiroga completed Banzer's term and laid the groundwork for the 2002 elections. The May 2002 presidential elections became a contest between former president Sánchez de Lozada and Evo Morales, an Aymara Indian and *cocalero* leader who headed the ticket of the Movement Toward Socialism (Movimiento Al Socialismo— MAS) party. In the bitterly fought race, Sánchez de Lozada prevailed by a slight margin. Sánchez de Lozada's second administration sought a continuation of his controversial capitalization program. However, the water war initiated a period of intense conflict between the social movements and the government, limiting the latter's ability to implement its policies. During 2002 and 2003, the government was increasingly challenged by the disruptive activities of the social movements. In September 2003, violent protests erupted in response to the government's plan to institute an income tax and to export liquefied natural gas to the United States by means of a pipeline through Chile. Approximately 80 demonstrators were killed in clashes with troops deployed to break up blockades of the highways. In October, mobs from the nearby shantytown of El Alto occupied and sacked government buildings in La Paz. In order to quell the violence, Sánchez de Lozada resigned and handed over the government to Vice President Carlos Mesa Gisbert.

Mesa's appointment as president temporarily eased the crisis but failed to resolve the dispute between the supporters and opponents of a foreign corporate role in the extraction and sale of natural gas. Mesa attempted to defuse the crisis by submitting the gas question to the public in a national referendum. The July 2004 referendum handed Mesa a tactical victory by approving the export of gas, albeit under greater state controls than originally anticipated. Despite a promising start, Mesa's administration was brought down in June 2005 by a new wave of road blockades and large-scale protests in La Paz. With the threat of a violent escalation looming, as well as talk of secession by the eastern provinces, Congress agreed on Eduardo Rodríguez Veltze, then serving as president of the Supreme Court, as interim president. Sworn in on June 10, 2005, Rodríguez immediately called for a special national election in December 2005.

The December 2005 elections were widely anticipated as an opportunity for Bolivians to end the "crisis of governance." In addition to the presidential, senatorial, and congressional races, Bolivians also would be voting for the first time for nine departmental governors (prefects). The prefectural elections were expected to produce a significant decentralization of political power—one of the few initiatives on which a majority of Bolivians could agree. The presidential contest became a two-candidate race between Evo Morales of the leftist MAS and former President Jorge "Tuto" Quiroga of the conservative Social Democratic Power (Poder Democrático y Social—Podemos) coalition. Despite concerns that neither candidate would win a clear-cut mandate, Morales was elected with 53.7 percent of the vote, becoming the first president of Indian ethnicity in Bolivia's history as well as the first majority president since the revolution. A high turnout of more than 80 percent of eligible voters lent added legitimacy to the results. The MAS's strong showing in the presidential race and in the Chamber of Deputies was counterbalanced by opposition control of the Senate and of a majority of the prefectures. In early 2006, the Morales administration's prospects for addressing Bolivia's myriad challenges were not yet known. Bolivia remained deeply divided by contending ethnic, class, and regional loyalties that would severely test the new administration's capacity to forge a national consensus on fundamental economic and political issues.

GEOGRAPHY

Location: Bolivia is located in Central South America, surrounded by Brazil to the north and east, Argentina and Paraguay to the south, and Peru and Chile to the west.

Size: Bolivia has a land area of 1,098,580 square kilometers—an area

Click to Enlarge Image

about three times the size of Montana. Bolivia ceded significant tracts of its territory through wars and negotiations. Its present size has been fixed since 1938. Bolivia is the fifth largest country in South America.

Land Boundaries: Bolivia has been landlocked since 1884. It shares borders with Argentina (832 kilometers), Brazil (3,400 kilometers), Chile (861 kilometers), Paraguay (750 kilometers), and Peru (900 kilometers).

Disputed Territory: Although treaties have officially resolved Bolivia's nineteenth-century border disputes, Bolivia continues to fight for a sovereign corridor to the Pacific through the Atacama Desert region it lost to Chile in the War of the Pacific.

Length of Coastline: None.

Maritime Claims: None.

Topography: Dramatic elevation changes distinguish Bolivian topography. La Paz, at 3,600 meters above sea level, is the world's highest capital city. The country is split into three topographical regions: the Andes and arid highlands of the west, the semi-tropical valleys in the middle third of the country, and the tropical lowlands of the east. Bolivia's high plateau, or altiplano, is located between the two major Andean mountain ranges—the Cordillera Occidental and the Cordillera Oriental. The altiplano is arid in the south but served by Lake Titicaca in the north. The country's highest mountain peak, Mt. Illiamani, southeast of La Paz, is more than 6,000 meters high. The lower, eastern slopes of the Cordillera Oriental, known as the Yungas, compose the semi-tropical region of the country. Rivers, plentiful in this region, drain into the Amazon Basin. By contrast, the Bolivian lowlands in the east, including the Chaco region, face semiarid conditions. Although forests cover nearly half of the country, the ample plains are used for cattle grazing and, in less inhabited regions, for coca cultivation.

Principal Rivers: Bolivia has more than 14,000 kilometers of navigable rivers. The Beni, Chapare, Desaguadero, Guaporé, Mamoré, Paraguay, and Pilcomayo form the country's major waterways. Plans have been finalized to widen and deepen the Paraguay River in order to improve access to the Atlantic.

Climate: Bolivia's extreme range of elevations gives the country a wide range of climates. Additionally, the El Niño weather phenomenon (occurring every three to seven years) affects Bolivia's climate. Generally speaking, the mountains of the southwest experience the coldest and driest weather. Conditions get warmer and wetter as one travels farther east. The Amazon Basin in the northeast floods during the rainy season while the plains region experiences extended droughts. The average temperature in the altiplano in the west, extending from Lake Titicaca south to the borders with Chile and Argentina, is 8° C. Because the country is south of the equator, Bolivia's winter falls in the middle of the calendar year.

Natural Resources: Bolivia's large tin deposits have shaped the country's recent economic history. Bolivia also has other mineral wealth, including large quantities of antimony, gold, iron, natural gas, petroleum, tungsten, and zinc. Bolivia's dense forests support a burgeoning timber industry, and its rivers produce hydropower.

Land Use: According to the Ministry of Agriculture, only 15 percent of Bolivia's land is suitable for agriculture. Of that arable land, just 12 percent is currently in use, with an additional 10 percent used for animal grazing. In the agricultural sector, Bolivia has focused on increasing yields through the use of new technology rather than on expanding agricultural acreage.

Environmental Factors: A land-use survey conducted in 2001 revealed a 6 percent loss of primary forest over the previous two decades. Even with this encroaching desertification, however, forests still cover more than 50 percent of Bolivian territory. Bolivia's history of slash-and-burn agriculture, overgrazing, and industrial pollution has caused significant concern among environmentalists. Soil erosion, made worse by seasonal flooding, and contaminated water supplies are Bolivia's most pressing environmental problems. The National Service for Protected Areas, established in 1998, currently manages 21 protected areas.

Time Zone: Bolivia operates four hours behind Greenwich Mean Time (GMT).

SOCIETY

Population: In 2004 Bolivia had an estimated population of nearly 9.3 million, with an annual population growth rate of 2.4 percent. Bolivia has low population density, only 8.5 people per square kilometer. In terms of geographic settlement, 42 percent of Bolivians live in the altiplano region in the west, followed by 30 percent in the eastern plains region and 29 percent in highland valleys in the central part of the country. Urbanization is low but rising. The urban population of the country is increasing at a rate of 3.6 percent annually, mostly as a result of the migration of rural residents to cities. In 2004 about 62 percent of Bolivians lived in cities, including 40 percent in cities with more than 200,000 inhabitants. La Paz, located in the altiplano, and Santa Cruz, in central Bolivia, are the most densely populated cities. Oruro, located in the altiplano southeast of La Paz, is Bolivia's fastest growing urban area.

Demography: Bolivia has a young and ethnically diverse population. Statistics show that 35 percent of the population is younger than 15, nearly 60 percent is 15–64, and only 4 percent is 65 and older. Experts estimate Bolivia's birthrate at nearly 23.8 births per 1,000. The infant mortality rate stands at 53 deaths per 1,000 live births and the child mortality rate at 66 deaths per 1,000 live births, while the overall death rate is 7.6 deaths per 1,000. Life expectancy in Bolivia, 65.5 years on average, is shorter than in most other South American countries.

Ethnic Groups and Languages: Ethnically, Bolivia is not dominated by any single group of people. In a survey conducted in 2001, the National Statistics Institute found the following breakdown: mestizo (mixed race), 30 percent; Quechua, 28 percent; Aymara, 19 percent; and European, 12 percent. The remaining 11 percent come from a collection of ethnicities. Spanish is spoken by 87 percent of the population. Quechua (34 percent) and Aymara are the other prominent languages.

Religion: The Roman Catholic Church has a dominant presence in Bolivia. An estimated 95 percent of Bolivians are Roman Catholic. The remaining 5 percent are Protestant. Bolivia's constitution mandates religious freedom, and the government has no record of suppressing any religious groups. However, some Catholic priests are supported by government pensions, in exchange for land that the church ceded to the government in the past. Only Roman Catholic religious instruction is provided in the country's public schools, but students are not required to attend religious sessions.

Education and Literacy: In education, as in many other areas of Bolivian life, a divide exists between Bolivia's rural and urban areas. Rural illiteracy levels remain high, even as the rest of the country becomes increasingly literate. This disparity stems partly from the fact that many children living in rural areas are forced to contribute economically to their family households and thus are much less likely to attend school. On average, children from rural areas attend school for 4.2 years, while children in urban areas receive an average of 9.4 years of education. A gender divide also exists. Females, on average, receive about 1.5 years less schooling than males. The female illiteracy rate is 19.6 percent while that for males is 7.4 percent. The country's illiteracy level as a whole, 13–14 percent, is higher than in other South American countries.

The problems with Bolivian education are not necessarily attributable to lack of funding. Bolivia devotes 23 percent of its annual budget to educational expenditures, a higher percentage than in most other South American countries, albeit from a smaller national budget. A comprehensive, seven-year plan of education reform has made some significant changes. Initiated in 1994, the plan decentralized educational funding in order to meet diverse local needs, improved teacher training and curricula, and changed the school grade system. Resistance from teachers' unions, however, has slowed implementation of some of the intended reforms.

Health: In terms of key health indicators, Bolivia ranks nearly last among the Western Hemisphere countries. Only Haiti scores consistently lower. Bolivia's child mortality rate of 66 per 1,000 live births is the worst in South America. Proper nourishment is a constant struggle for many Bolivians. Experts estimate that 7 percent of Bolivian children under the age of five and 23 percent of the entire population suffer from malnutrition.

Bolivians living in rural areas lack proper sanitation and medical services, rendering many helpless against still potent diseases such as malaria (in tropical areas) and Chagas' disease. Statistics indicate that only 20 percent of the rural population in Bolivia has access to safe water and sanitation. The prevalence of human immunodeficiency virus/acquired immune deficiency syndrome (HIV/AIDS) in Bolivia appears to be low, around 0.1 percent of the population. Between 1984 and 2002, only 333 cases of AIDS were reported to United Nations officials.

Bolivia's health care system is in the midst of reform, funded in part by international organizations such as the World Bank. The number of physicians practicing in Bolivia has doubled in recent years, to about 130 per 100,000 citizens, a comparable ratio for the region. Current priorities include providing basic health care to more women and children, expanding immunization, and tackling the problems of diarrhea and tuberculosis, which are leading causes of death among children. As a percentage of its national budget, Bolivia's health care expenditures are 4.3 percent, also on a par with regional norms. However, its annual per capita spending of US$145 is lower than in most South American countries.

Welfare: Among developing nations, as defined by the United Nations (UN), Bolivia ranks twenty-seven according to the Human Poverty Index. Overall, Bolivia ranked 114 out of 175 on the UN Human Development Index in 2002. Despite efforts at reform, Bolivia's economic development has been continually hindered by political unrest, a lack of economic diversification, and the extremely profitable, but internationally condemned, illegal drug trade. By some estimates, nearly 65 percent of Bolivians live in poverty. That number rises to 80 percent when considering only Bolivia's rural population. Annually, the World Bank designates up to US$150 million to bolster Bolivia's economy and infrastructure.

Bolivia first implemented a social security program in 1959. Workers aged 65 years or older who retire from jobs in the "formal" sector of the economy receive a pension from the Bolivian government. However, in 1997 Bolivia followed the trend of other Latin American countries and privatized the system. Currently, Bolivian formal-sector workers are required to deposit 10 percent of their salary into a private social insurance program. Employers contribute an additional 2 percent of the worker's regular salary. Except for those workers who retired under the previous system, there is no guaranteed minimum old-age pension, but any unused accumulated capital is payable to an heir on the death of the insured. In addition to retirement, Bolivia has social welfare to help those disabled, both long-term and short-term, and women who become pregnant. Limited funds are also available to aid the unemployed, underemployed, and families in need of assistance, but it is likely that stated benefits differ from actual payments.

ECONOMY

Overview: Bolivia's economic history reveals a pattern of a single-commodity focus. From silver to tin to coca, Bolivia has enjoyed only occasional periods of economic diversification. Political instability and difficult topography have constrained efforts to modernize the agricultural sector. Similarly, relatively low population growth coupled with low life expectancy has kept the labor supply in flux and prevented industries from flourishing. Rampant inflation and corruption also have thwarted development. The mining industry, especially the extraction of natural gas and zinc, currently dominates Bolivia's export economy.

Gross Domestic Product (GDP): Bolivia had an estimated GDP of US$22.3 billion in 2004, with a growth rate from the previous year of 3.7 percent.

Government Budget: Bolivia experienced a budget deficit of about US$500 million in 2004. Expenditures were nearly US$2.8 billion while revenues amounted to only about US$2.3 billion.

Inflation: Inflation has plagued, and at times crippled, the Bolivian economy since the 1970s. At one time in 1985, Bolivia experienced an inflation rate of more than 20,000 percent. Fiscal and monetary reform reduced the inflation rate to single digits by the 1990s, and in 2004 Bolivia experienced a manageable 4.9 percent rate of inflation.

Agriculture, Forestry, and Fishing: Agriculture, forestry, and fishing accounted for 14 percent of Bolivia's gross domestic product (GDP) in 2003, down from 28 percent in 1986. Combined, these activities employ nearly 44 percent of Bolivia's workers. Most agricultural workers are engaged in subsistence farming—the dominant economic activity of the highlands region. Agricultural production in Bolivia is complicated by both the country's topography and climate. High elevations make farming difficult, as do the El Niño weather patterns and seasonal flooding. Bolivia's agricultural GDP continues to rise but has attained only a rather modest average growth rate of 2.8 percent annually since 1991.

Bolivia's most lucrative agricultural product continues to be coca, of which Bolivia is currently the world's third largest cultivator. The Bolivian government, in response to international pressure, has worked to restrict coca cultivation for the use of producing cocaine. However, eradication efforts have been hampered by the lack of a suitable replacement crop for rural communities that have cultivated coca for generations. Since 2001, Bolivia's leading legal agricultural export has been soybeans. Additionally, cotton, coffee, and sugarcane have been viable exports for Bolivia. For domestic consumption, corn, wheat, and potatoes are the crops of choice of Bolivian farmers.

Despite its vast forests, Bolivia has only a minor timber industry. In 2003 timber accounted for only 3.5 percent of export earnings. The Forestry Law of 1996 imposed a tax on sawn timber and consequently cut Bolivian timber exports significantly. The tax was used to establish the Forestry Stewardship Council, which has been only minimally successful in forest restoration efforts and eliminating illegal logging. With increased efficiency, Bolivia could likely expand the profitability of its forest resources, while still protecting them from overexploitation.

Bolivia has a small fishing industry that taps the country's freshwater lakes and streams. The annual catch averages about 6,000 tons.

Mining and Minerals: Mining continues to be vital to Bolivia's economy. The collapse of the world tin market in the 1980s led to a restructuring of the industry. The state dramatically reduced its control and presently operates only a small portion of mining activities. Small-scale operations, often with low productivity, employ many former state miners. Natural gas has supplanted tin and silver as the country's most valuable natural commodity. A discovery in 1997 confirmed a tenfold gain in Bolivia's known natural gas reserves. Finding markets to utilize this resource, both domestically and internationally, has been slowed by a lack of infrastructure and conflicts over the state's role in controlling natural resources.

Although the world tin market has reemerged, Bolivia now faces stiff competition from Southeast Asian countries producing lower-cost alluvial tin. Gold and silver production has increased dramatically over the past decade. Annually, as of 2002 Bolivia extracted and exported more than 11,000 kilograms of gold and 461 tons of silver. Additionally, Bolivia has increased zinc production, extracting more than 100,000 tons each year. Other metals excavated include antimony, iron, and tungsten.

Industry and Manufacturing: Annually, manufacturing has accounted for approximately 18 percent of Bolivia's gross domestic product since 1995. Most industry is small-scale, aimed at regional markets rather than national operations. Inadequate credit options and competition from the black market have kept Bolivia's manufacturing sector from developing fully. Leading manufactured goods in Bolivia include textiles, clothing, non-durable consumer goods, processed soya, refined metals, and refined petroleum.

Energy: Bolivia is energy self-sufficient. The country's energy needs are relatively small but growing consistently. Bolivia uses oil for the majority of its power needs, followed by natural gas. The country has large reserves of both. Bolivia's energy sector changed significantly when the government allowed privatization in the mid-1990s. International companies quickly invested in Bolivian energy sources, particularly in natural gas, and made Bolivia into a player in the world energy market.

The exportation of Bolivian energy resources, while potentially lucrative economically, has been politically hazardous. President Gonzalo Sánchez de Lozada ultimately resigned over his plan to export natural gas to the United States and Mexico in 2003. Subsequent politicians have been hesitant to act decisively even though Bolivia's economy could readily use an export boost. On June 6, 2005, President Carlos Mesa offered his resignation to the Bolivian Congress after months of demonstrations by Bolivia's Indian population calling for renationalizing the natural gas and oil sectors. Mesa had increased taxation on foreign companies while still encouraging their investment in Bolivian energy development.

Bolivia has estimated oil reserves of 441 million barrels, the fifth largest in South America. The country's natural gas reserves total 27.6 trillion cubic feet according to Bolivian government figures, ranking Bolivia behind only Venezuela in terms of proven natural gas reserves in South America. Additionally, Bolivia produces more electricity with its nine power companies than it can consume. In 2002 Bolivia generated 4.1 billion kilowatt-hours of electricity but consumed only 3.8 billion kilowatt-hours.

Services: The services industry in Bolivia remains undeveloped. Inhabiting one of the poorest countries in South America, Bolivians have weak purchasing power. The retail sector suffers from weak demand and competition with a large black market of contraband goods. U.S. companies such as McDonald's and Domino's have pulled out of Bolivia in recent years.

Banking and Finance: Banking in Bolivia has long suffered from corruption and weak regulation. However, a series of reforms initiated by the 1993 Banking Law and subsequent acts are gradually improving Bolivia's banking sector. Bolivia has a Central Bank and nine private banks. Consolidation occurred following reforms, lowering the number of private banks in Bolivia from 14 in 1995 to nine in 2003. Foreign participation and investment in Bolivian banks are allowed.

About 90 percent of Bolivian bank deposits are held in U.S. dollars. The Bolivian government is trying to change this situation by taxing dollarized accounts while exempting boliviano accounts from the tax. As recently as 2002, 27 percent of all loans were non-performing, leading most foreign investors to focus their resources in the somewhat-safer venue of corporate lending. Most bank lending in 2003 went to manufacturing (24 percent), followed by property services (18 percent) and trade and retail (16 percent). Bad debt remains at a historically high level. Further reforms are necessary, including the pending act to introduce a deposit guarantee system.

Bolivia's stock market expanded in 1998 to include corporate bonds, along with the money market and government bond options that had existed previously. The privatization of Bolivia's social security program has bolstered the stock market.

Tourism: Bolivia's spectacular vistas and natural attractions have not been enough to transform the country into a major tourist destination because of its political instability and lack of first-class accommodations. Still, Bolivia's tourist industry has grown gradually over the past 15 years. In 2000 Bolivia attracted 306,000 tourists, compared with 254,000 in 1990. Tourist revenue peaked at US$179 million in 1999. Tourism in Bolivia declined following the September 11, 2001, attack on the United States, as was the case across North and South America.

Labor: The economic downturn of the late 1990s, coupled with privatization and austerity efforts led by President Mesa, resulted in significant unemployment. Although the Bolivian government does not keep unemployment statistics, outside experts estimate unemployment to be between 8 and 10 percent of the population. Underemployment of Bolivia's workforce of nearly 4 million is also widespread. As a result of the lack of formal employment opportunities, nearly 65 percent of the urban workforce was self-employed in 2002.

Labor unions have a strong history in Bolivia. Many workers in the formal sector belong to unions. The larger unions, such as the Bolivian Labor Federation and the Trade Union Federation of Bolivian Mine Workers, have been successful in rallying workers to countless strikes and work stoppages. Nevertheless, working conditions for most Bolivian workers are difficult.

Foreign Economic Relations: Bolivia was a founding member of the Andean Group, a South American organization designed to promote trade among Bolivia, Colombia, Ecuador, Peru, and Venezuela. Subsequently renamed the Andean Community (Comunidad Andina—CAN), the organization has succeeded in increasing intra-South American trade. Trade among member countries rose from US$3.6 billion in 1991 to US$10.3 billion in 2003. Bolivia also belongs to the Common Market of the South (Mercado Común del Sur—Mercosur). Bolivia became an associate member in 1997 in order to open investment opportunities with the founding Mercosur countries (Argentina, Brazil, Paraguay, and Uruguay), as well as other Mercosur associate members (Chile, Colombia, Ecuador, Peru, and Venezuela). Bolivia conducted more than US$1 billion in trade with Mercosur countries in 2003. As a result of negotiations initiated in 1999 on a possible South American Free Trade Area (SAFTA), the two groups announced in December 2004 that they would merge, creating a South American Community of Nations patterned after the European Union.

Imports: Bolivian imports of goods and services were valued at about US$2.1 billion in 2004. The import of consumer goods increased for the first time since 2002. By sector, Bolivia imported mostly intermediate goods, followed by industrial, capital, and consumer goods. Leading sources of Bolivian imports include Brazil, Argentina, the United States, and Chile.

Exports: Bolivian exports of goods and services in 2004 stood at more than US$2.1 billion compared with US$1.9 billion in 2003. Increased production of hydrocarbons, especially natural gas, led Bolivia's trade upturn in 2004. A 20-year supply contract with Brazil for natural gas, ending in 2019, has provided the necessary capital to increase production. In 2004 export revenues for natural gas topped US$619 million. Bolivia also exported significant quantities of petroleum. Beyond hydrocarbons, other significant exports included zinc, soya, iron ore, and tin. In 2001 Brazil overtook the United States as Bolivia's primary export outlet. Switzerland, Venezuela, and Colombia are also important export partners. Bolivia has actively sought to foster economic connections in South America after long relying on the United States as its primary trade partner.

Trade Balance: Bolivia had an estimated trade surplus of more than US$340 million in 2004. This figure represents a marked change in Bolivia's economic balance sheet. Bolivia reached a peak trade deficit of US$888 million in 1998 before increased hydrocarbon exports radically altered the situation.

Balance of Payments: Bolivia had a large negative balance of payments for 2002—US$317 million. However, this situation has been remedied by the vast increase in export revenue. Estimates for the balance of payments for 2004 show a record surplus of US$126 million.

External Debt: Bolivia's external debt totaled an estimated US$5.7 billion in 2004. The International Monetary Fund has assisted Bolivia in paying down this debt. In 1995 the United States, among other countries, reduced Bolivia's debt by two-thirds.

Foreign Investment: Foreign investment in Bolivia was buoyed in 1995 by privatization. Investment in mining and natural gas extraction increased, as did investment in the banking sector. However, the economic decline of the late 1990s, along with political unrest, caused foreign investors to pull out of Bolivia once again. In 2000 foreign investors contributed US$736 million to the Bolivian economy. In 2002 this total fell to US$676 million.

Foreign Aid: Bolivia depends on foreign aid to fund its improvement projects and to service its large external debt. In 1998 the World Bank and International Monetary Fund awarded Bolivia a debt-relief package worth US$760 million. Bolivia also has received relief under the World Bank's Heavily Indebted Poor Countries program, which, if Bolivia meets all checkpoints, will total US$1.2 billion by 2011. In 2004 the United States designated more than US$150 million for assistance to Bolivia.

Currency and Exchange Rate: Bolivia's currency is the boliviano (BOB). The exchange rate in January 2006 was about 8 bolivianos per US$1.

Fiscal Year: Calendar year.

TRANSPORTATION AND TELECOMMUNICATIONS

Overview: Bolivia's extreme terrain and elevation changes make cross-country transportation difficult. Flooding and landslides also cause problems. Because Bolivia is landlocked, the oceans offer no aid in moving commodities, and export costs are higher for Bolivia than for most other countries in South America.

Roads: Bolivia has more than 60,000 kilometers of roads. Only 4,000 kilometers of that total, however, are paved. A transportation improvement plan calls for the country to double the length of paved roads by 2006. Ongoing improvement projects include a highway between Santa Cruz and the Brazilian border at Puerto Suárez and another between La Paz and the Brazilian border at Guayaramerín.

Railroads: Bolivia's railroad network extends nearly 4,300 kilometers. However, rather than one unified network, separate networks exist in the eastern lowlands and the western highlands. The eastern network connects the Santa Cruz region with both Argentina at La Quiaca and Brazil at Corumbá. The western network connects with Chilean rail centers. Currently, plans exist for a railroad connecting Santa Cruz and Cochabamba. The feasibility and funding for this improvement are under debate. The Bolivian government owned the country's largest railroad company, Empresa Nacional de Ferrocarriles, until 1995, when it was capitalized.

Ports: The river port Puerto Aguirre, at the border with Brazil on the Paraguay River, functions as Bolivia's primary outlet to international waters. In addition, Bolivia has free port privileges in Argentina (Rosario), Brazil (Belém, Corumbá, Porto Velho, and Santos), Chile (Arica), Paraguay, and Peru (Ilo).

Inland Waterways: Bolivia has more than 14,000 kilometers of navigable rivers. The Paraguay River functions as the country's primary conduit for trade.

Civil Aviation and Airports: Bolivia has more than 1,000 airports spread throughout its territory. Only 16 of these airports, however, have paved runways. The vast majority are rural airstrips. La Paz (El Alto) and Santa Cruz (Viru-Viru) are home to the country's two international airports. Two airlines dominate domestic travel in Bolivia. Lloyd Aéreo Boliviano services most of Bolivia's major towns. The state ceded control of the airline in 1995, and now private investors control part of the company. Aerosur, based in Santa Cruz, serves as the country's other dominant air service provider. Because La Paz is at such a high elevation, large airliners cannot take off from there at full capacity. Most flights from the capital city stop over in Santa Cruz for more passengers or cargo before proceeding to their final destination.

Pipelines: Bolivia has more than 9,000 kilometers of pipelines, with the majority being used to transport natural gas. Bolivia has 4,860 kilometers of pipeline for natural gas, 2,457 kilometers for oil, 1,589 kilometers for refined products, and 47 kilometers for liquid petroleum gas. Some experts maintain that inadequate infrastructure, including pipelines, has prevented Bolivia from taking full economic advantage of its natural resources. Bolivia currently has cross-border natural gas pipelines into Argentina and Brazil.

Telecommunications: The telecommunications industry has expanded and diversified since privatization in 1995. The Empresa Nacional de Telecomunicaciones (known as Entel) was purchased by an Italian company and subsequently expanded and improved to offer better service across the country. In 2001 the telecommunications market opened for full competition, and one company (Viva) created a separate network to challenge Entel's holdings. Although Entel still dominates the market, service, quality and price all have improved to benefit the consumer since 1993. Nevertheless, bureaucratic difficulties still confront many Bolivians trying to establish new telephone service.

Bolivia's telecommunications development, in comparison with other South American countries, is still relatively limited. Bolivia has 63 fixed telephone lines and 94 cellular subscribers per 1,000 people. Only 2 percent of Bolivians, compared with 3.6 percent regionally, have access to a personal computer. Bolivia has only 21 Internet users per 1,000 people, compared with 76 in Peru, for example. Nevertheless, access to the Internet and the number of Internet users have grown significantly each year. From 2001 to 2002, the number of Internet users in Bolivia increased from 180,000 to 270,000.

GOVERNMENT AND POLITICS

Political System: Bolivia is a unitary democratic republic, empowered by the revised constitution of 1994. Similar to the United States, Bolivia has executive, legislative, and judicial branches of government. The directly elected president serves a five-year term and appoints an executive cabinet. Traditionally, the president has been a strong executive, responsible for foreign diplomacy, setting economic policy, and commanding the armed forces, among other duties. The president cannot be reelected to successive terms.

The bicameral Congress consists of a 27-member Senate and a 130-member Chamber of Deputies and is limited to debating and approving legislation initiated by the executive. Congress meets annually for a session of 90 working days. At the request of the executive or a majority of its members, Congress may expand its annual session to 120 days or convene extraordinary sessions to debate specific legislation. Each of the nine departments elects three senators. About one-half of the members serving in the Chamber of Deputies are directly elected, while the other representatives gain their seats through indirect party nominations. All members of Congress serve five-year terms.

Bolivia's judicial system consists of a Supreme Court, district (or superior) courts in each of the nine departments, and provincial and local courts to try minor cases. The 12 Supreme Court justices, nominated by the president and confirmed by the Congress, serve non-renewable 10-year terms. The Supreme Court is divided into four chambers of three justices each, with two chambers dealing with civil cases, another dealing with criminal cases, and the fourth with administrative, social, and mining cases. The superior courts hear appeals of lower-court decisions and review the application of Bolivian law. The Supreme Court hears only cases involving exceptional circumstances. A Constitutional Tribunal handles appeals on constitutional issues. Both the superior courts and the Supreme Court have the right to alter the sentences or negate the decisions of lower courts. Although the judiciary is meant to be independent of outside influence, political pressure and judicial corruption have long been present in Bolivia. Reforms in 1998 added several components to the judicial system in an effort to curtail corruption, including an independent judicial council to oversee and investigate the conduct of judges and a public defender program.

Administrative Divisions: In 1989 the Congress divided Bolivia into its present administrative form, consisting of nine departments. In descending order of population size, the departments are: La Paz, Santa Cruz, Cochabamba, Potosí, Chuquisaca, Oruro, Tarija, Beni, and Pando.

Provincial and Local Government: Bolivia's nine regional departments are divided into 94 provinces, which are further divided into 312 municipalities. The highest executive authority in a department is the prefect—roughly comparable to a state governor in the United States. As a result of constitutional reforms ratified in 1995, in December 2005 the nine departmental prefects were directly elected by voters, replacing the previous system of presidential appointment of prefects. Sub-prefects administer provinces. Bolivian towns and cities directly elect mayors and municipal councils. Municipal elections occur every five years.

Judicial and Legal System: Bolivia's legal system is based on Spanish law and the Napoleonic Code. The 1999 penal code also incorporated the customary law of indigenous peoples. The implementation of the Code of Criminal Procedures (CCP) in May 2002 improved Bolivia's court system. Members of the Judicial Technical Police, lawyers, law students, judges, and nongovernmental organization (NGO) representatives have received training in the new CCP, emphasizing the protection of legal and human rights. With the goal of rooting out corruption, the CCP changed the criminal justice system from a closed, written system to one with open, oral trials. Additionally, the Public Ministry Law, enacted in March 2002, introduced the role of prosecutor in the Bolivian legal system. Rather than the judge leading the investigation against a defendant, prosecutors now conduct the state's inquiry.

In misdemeanor cases, a defendant appears in the lower courts before only a judge. In felony cases, two judges and a jury of three citizens decide the defendant's fate. Defendants have the right to an attorney, to remain silent, to due process, and to a presumption of innocence, among others rights. In practice, these rights are often ignored. Nevertheless, the new transparency brought with the CCP has made the rights of the defendant somewhat easier to defend.

Electoral System: Since 1982, Bolivian elections have produced largely peaceful exchanges of political power. Elections for national and municipal offices are held every five years. Universal and compulsory suffrage exists in Bolivia (at age 21, or age 18 if married), but citizens must produce documentation in order to vote. Electoral judges serve in each department in order to rule on contested voter eligibility and other election discrepancies. Election fraud historically has plagued Bolivia, and accusations of fraud are a part of the Bolivian electoral system.

Politics and Political Parties: Bolivia has a fragmented political party system, as evidenced by the multitude of parties represented in the Congress. Support for the traditionally dominant parties—the Nationalist Revolutionary Movement (Movimiento Nacionalista Revolucionario—MNR), Nationalist Democratic Action (Acción Democrático Nacionalista—ADN), and Movement of the Revolutionary Left (Movimiento de la Izquierda

Revolucionaria—MIR)—has declined since the 1980s. In their place, a plethora of single-interest parties have arisen. Regional and ethnic loyalties have replaced national coalitions. This development has led to a series of alliances among seemingly disparate political parties. For example, in 2002 four presidential candidates each received more than 15 percent of the vote, led by Gonzalo Sánchez de Lozada with 23 percent. This result triggered a runoff between Sánchez de Lozada and the second-place candidate, Evo Morales. Sánchez de Lozada prevailed in this contest, but only by securing the support of his former rivals and forming an impossible-to-maintain four-party coalition. The power sharing required in such a political atmosphere has severely curtailed the effectiveness of the Congress. Patronage is divided among the parties to such an extent that bureaucratic efficiency also is compromised.

Carlos Mesa, a political independent, resigned from the presidency on June 6, 2005, as a result of massive public demonstrations in La Paz and out of frustration over Bolivia's deadlocked political system. Eduardo Rodríguez succeeded Mesa on an interim basis, and a special national election was held in December 2005. Bolivians went to the polls in December 2005 to elect a president, both houses of Congress, and the nine departmental prefects. The top presidential candidates were Jorge "Tuto" Quiroga, former president and leader of the conservative ADN party, now associated with the Social Democratic Power (Poder Democrático y Social—Podemas) coalition; Evo Morales, indigenous leader of the leftist Movement Toward Socialism (Movimiento al Socialismo—MAS) party; and wealthy businessman Samuel Doria Medina of the centrist National Unity (Unidad Nacional—UN) party.

Evo Morales won the December 2005 presidential election in a landslide victory with 53.7 percent of the vote, thus making him the first ethnic Indian president in Bolivia's history and the first president elected by a majority since the 1952 revolution. The controversial indigenous leader campaigned on a platform of nationalizing the hydrocarbons sector and ending a coca eradication program supported by the United States. The MAS's strong showing in the presidential race and in the Chamber of Deputies was counterbalanced by opposition control of the Senate and of a majority of the nine prefectures.

Mass Media: Bolivia has nearly 200 privately owned television stations, but because rural regions of the country have few televisions and television reception is poor in many areas of the country, radio remains an important news disseminator. At last count, Bolivia had more than 480 radio stations, most of which were regional in scope. Bolivia also has eight national newspapers, in addition to many local ones. Of the national papers, four are based in La Paz, three in Santa Cruz, and one in Cochabamba. Most Bolivians continue to get their news from newspapers and radio broadcasts.

The Bolivian constitution protects freedom of the press and speech. Most newspapers take antigovernment positions. Both state-owned and privately owned radio stations operate without government censorship. Some restrictions do exist, however. The Penal Code demands jail time for those persons found guilty of slandering, insulting, or defaming public officials. In particular, the president, vice president, and ministers are protected by the Penal Code. Those charged with violating press standards are brought before the independent La Paz Press Tribunal.

Foreign Relations: Bolivia traditionally has had strong ties to the United States. Economically, the United States has been a long-standing consumer of Bolivian exports and a partner in development projects. Bolivia is heavily dependent on foreign aid. The country receives about US$500 million each year from 18 foreign institutions, including about US$150 million from the United States. In 1991 the United States forgave more than US$350 million owed by Bolivia to the U.S. Agency for International Development and the U.S. Department of Agriculture. Presently, about one-third of U.S. aid to Bolivia is earmarked for anti-drug trafficking programs.

More recently, Bolivia has attempted to strengthen its ties with neighboring South American countries. A bilateral agreement for natural gas exports with Argentina in 2004 represented a significant step in overcoming past hostilities to establish a mutually beneficial relationship. Bolivia's diplomatic relationship with Chile remains strained, simmering still from the loss of Bolivia's entire coastline to Chile in the late nineteenth century. Diplomatic relations between the two countries, reestablished briefly between 1975 and 1978, have been broken off at the ambassadorial level.

Membership in International Organizations: Bolivia is a member of the United Nations and many of its affiliated organizations. Regionally, Bolivia belongs to the Amazon Pact, Andean Community, Latin American Integration Association, Organization of American States, Common Market of the South (Mercosur), and Rio Group. Bolivia is also a member of the International Monetary Fund, International Parliamentary Union, International Telecommunications Satellite Organization, Non-Aligned Movement, World Health Organization, and World Trade Organization.

Major International Treaties: Bolivia is a party to many significant treaties, including international agreements on biological weapons, chemical weapons, copyright, human rights, intellectual property, nuclear weapons non-proliferation, and torture. In the environmental arena, Bolivia is a party to the following agreements: Biodiversity, Climate Change (including the Kyoto Protocol), Desertification, Endangered Species, Hazardous Wastes, Law of the Sea, Marine Dumping, Ozone Layer Protection, Ship Pollution, Tropical Timber 83 and 94, and Wetlands.

NATIONAL SECURITY

Armed Forces Overview: Although its political history has been dominated by military coups, Bolivia's armed forces are relatively small and undeveloped. Bolivia currently has secure borders and few international threats, in comparison with previous times in its history. Efforts to reform and modernize the Bolivian armed forces have been suppressed as a result of the need to retain the support of the military establishment and because of more pressing political and civil issues. In spite of its weakness on the world scale, the Bolivian military historically has been the only institution that can maintain law and order in the country.

Foreign Military Relations: Bolivia receives military aid from the United States for its continuing fight against illicit drug production and trade. Bolivia and the United States have conducted joint training exercises, and Bolivia has received training funds through the

International Military Education and Training (IMET) program. Military relations with regional neighbors remain stable, but tensions between Peru and Chile have the potential to unbalance the military equilibrium currently governing South America. Bolivia opposes most Chilean interests as a result of lingering resentment over the War of the Pacific (1879–80).

External Threats: Since losing territory to Chile and Paraguay through military conflict in the early twentieth century, Bolivia has remained relatively safe from international threats. Internal riots and resistance represent a much more significant threat to Bolivian stability than do external threats.

Defense Budget: In 2004 Bolivia devoted US$132 million to military expenditures. Bolivia ranks near the bottom third of world countries in terms of both military spending and military expenditures as a percentage of GDP.

Major Military Units: Bolivia has three military services—the army, air force, and navy. The army has the majority of the military manpower, with 25,000 troops of the 31,500 in the Bolivian armed forces. The army is divided into six military divisions and includes a presidential guard infantry unit. The army still includes five horse-riding cavalry groups, along with one motorized cavalry group, one assault cavalry group, two airborne regiments, two mechanized infantry regiments, three motorized infantry regiments, six artillery regiments, six engineer battalions, and 21 infantry battalions. The 3,000-member air force is organized in two fighter squadrons; other squadrons are devoted to helicopters, weapons training, survey, air defense, and transport. Bolivia's navy has 3,500 personnel, 1,700 of whom are marines. Without ocean access, Bolivia's navy focuses on the country's rivers and Lake Titicaca. Six naval districts cover the country. One battalion of marines operates in each of the six districts.

Major Military Equipment: Much of Bolivia's military equipment is outdated. The army inventory includes 36 SK–105 Kuerassier light tanks, 24 Cascavel reconnaissance vehicles, and 59 armored personnel carriers. In terms of artillery, the army has 75-, 105-, and 122-millimeter towed guns. Additionally, the army has 81-millimeter and 107-millimeter mortars. Bolivia's air force makes use of an aged fleet of planes. Presently, it has 37 combat aircraft and 16 armed helicopters. Bolivia's fighter squadrons fly 18 AT–33AN fighter jets and 19 PC–7s. For transport and surveillance, a collection of Cessnas, Learjets, Saberliners, and King Air aircraft are used. Bolivia's naval fleet consists of 60 riverine and 18 support craft.

Military Service: Military service is voluntary unless enlistments fail to meet government quotas, which has been the case in recent history. More than half (20,000) of Bolivia's active troops are conscripted. Males become eligible for voluntary service at 18 but may be conscripted as young as 14. According to one estimate, nearly 40 percent of military personnel are less than 18 years of age. Active members of the armed services serve for periods of one year.

Paramilitary Forces: Bolivia's paramilitary force is larger than its armed forces. More than 31,000 national police officers and 6,000 narcotics police officers serve Bolivia's citizenry. The national police force is divided into nine brigades, two rapid response regiments, and 27 frontier units. Political instability and frequent civil unrest have made the paramilitary forces vital to Bolivia's well-being.

Foreign Military Forces: In the 1980s, the U.S. military collaborated with Bolivian forces to attempt to eradicate drug production. Public outcries against the presence of U.S. military forces, however, led to the withdrawal of U.S. forces. Currently, no foreign forces reside in Bolivia.

Military Forces Abroad: Bolivia plays a limited role in international peacekeeping. In 2004 Bolivia sent 207 troops the Democratic Republic of the Congo to participate in peacekeeping operations. Additionally, Bolivia sent observers to United Nations operations in Côte d'Ivoire, East Timor, Haiti, Liberia, Serbia and Montenegro, and Sierra Leone.

Police: Bolivia has a national police force of 31,000 officers that is responsible for internal security and maintaining law and order. Unlike in most Latin American countries, the Bolivian police force always has been responsible to the national government rather than to state or local officials. The 1950 Organic Law of Police and Carabineers officially separated the police from the military. Frequently, however, the national police call upon the military for assistance in quelling riots and civil protests.

Internal Threat: Bolivia has internal conflicts stemming from a variety of sources. Coca farmers resisting government efforts at crop eradication frequently have resorted to protest and violence against national police forces. In 2003 coca farmers and Bolivian troops clashed repeatedly, leaving more than 60 dead. Similarly, indigenous groups have organized in opposition to the perceived injustice of exporting natural gas for the primary benefit of large companies. And more generally, Bolivia's long-term poverty has produced instability and a rift between rural and urban communities. Although democratic participation is present in Bolivia, the fragmented political parties frequently serve as instigators of internal divisions rather than as functional outlets for varying opinions.

Terrorism: Bolivia is a signatory to the Inter-American Convention Against Terrorism and the Asunción Declaration of 2003, which unites Latin American countries to fight alongside the Colombian government against terrorism and drug trafficking. Despite its meager military budget, Bolivia has been one of the United States' most reliable South American partners in the war on terrorism. Bolivia has shared financial information with the United States regarding suspected terrorists in the country. In 2004 Bolivia established a counterterrorism coordination unit to bring together police, military, and diplomatic leaders.

Bolivia's efforts to eradicate the coca industry have been modestly successful. Increased pressure on coca farmers, however, has resulted in heightened domestic conflict and opened new possibilities for cooperation with terrorist organizations. Bolivia's varied topography and porous borders make the country a possible haven for terrorist groups. However, no major terrorist actions have taken place on Bolivian soil, and there is no evidence of the presence of international terrorist organizations in the country.

Human Rights: Bolivia is in accord with general human rights standards. It affords its citizens freedom of the press, speech, religion, and assembly. Those accused of committing crimes in Bolivia enjoy the right to a trial by jury and to legal representation. Although the judiciary operates independently, low pay makes many judges susceptible to bribes. Prisoners do not enjoy equal treatment. Those with money are able to buy larger cells and more food than those without access to funds.

Bolivians enjoy the right to vote in regular political elections and to assemble for political protests. Oftentimes, however, political protests have devolved into violence, and military and police forces have used violent measures to restore order. Bolivian political parties range from extreme conservative to extreme liberal, and citizens are unrestricted in joining the political party of their choice. Additionally, Bolivian workers have the right to unionize. About 25 percent of workers employed in the formal work sector belong to unions. A minimum wage and workweek standards exist, but enforcement has proved difficult.

Abuse of women and children is widespread and often unreported in Bolivia. Family violence, when reported, results in only a few days in jail and a small fine. The punishment for rape has become more severe in recent years. Those convicted of rape, including statutory rape, face significant jail time. However, a victim must press charges in order for rape to be a crime. Economic scarcity has led to human trafficking and child labor in Bolivia. Prostitution is legal in Bolivia, but many Bolivian women are taken against their will to other countries and forced to work in prostitution for little compensation. Children are often trafficked for labor. The Bolivian government, in cooperation with the United Nations, is working to curb abuse of Bolivian women and children both within Bolivia and abroad.